101 JOB INTERVIEW QUESTIONS

ANDREA MASALA

About the Author

My name is Andrea, and I was born in the late 80s in Cagliari-Italy.

After being a diligent student at school, I decided to study Languages and Communication at the University because I wanted to be able to speak with as many people as possible.

Then, I chose to specialize in International HR Management since I've always also enjoyed leading people to achieve their goals, so I enrolled in a University Master's.

During my student years and at the beginning of my professional career, I travelled quite a lot; I lived in Riga, Warsaw, Milan, Dubai, Turin, and Cracow.

After 5 years of living abroad, I realized there is no place like home, especially when you had the luck to be born on a wonderful Mediterranean island, Sardinia. Therefore, I came back and started working remotely.

With a total of 10 years of working experience as a Recruiter with some top multinationals (Siemens -

General Motors — Primark — Microsoft — GlaxoSmithKline — Nestlé), I learned all their HR and Recruitment secrets, I also had the opportunity to achieve 3 promotions up to becoming a People Manager, but I wasn't satisfied or fulfilled.

Thus, I chose to risk it all, resign, and go back to study again to perfect my Career Guidance and Professional Orientation skills with a second Master and I became an entrepreneur.

I founded Career Formulas.

Career Formulas is a project of different branches to help people find their space in the complex job market:

- Video consultancy
- Newsletter
- Blog
- Online courses
- Books
- Podcasts

Now I'm truly happy because, despite all the challenges, I do what I enjoy the most, helping people achieve more!

Contents

I. About the Author
II. Process and its steps
III. People and roles
IV. Preparation before the interviews
V. Behavioural vs technical examination
VI. ATS & virtual interviews
VII. The 101 questions
   i. Kick-off
   ii. Behavioural
   iii. Culture fit

- iv. Leadership
- v. Career aspirations
- vi. Technical skills
- vii. Tricky
- viii. Closing
- ix. Embarrassing

VIII. Salary negotiation

IX. Last recommendation

X. Bibliography

XI. Websites

XII. My links

Process and its steps

Job interview

noun [C] HR

UK / dʒə́wb ɪ́ntəvjɨw

**A meeting in which
an Employer asks the person applying for a job
question to see whether they would be
the right person to do that job:**

Go for / attend / conduct a job interview | *He'd been
for several job interviews but hadn't
been offered a job yet.*

This is the official definition of a *job interview* by the Cambridge Dictionary. Noticed anything?

Even the estimated team of Cambridge researchers chose to give you an example of its use in a sentence where the subject, the candidate, is struggling to get a job!

Hilarious, eh? Yes, maybe a bit, but honestly scarier.

If you bought this book, most probably you found yourself in a similar situation or perhaps, you're trying to anticipate it.

Well, let me tell you, you did the right thing.

I'm going to unveil to you all the secrets of a perfect job interview.

The first thing you have to know is the process and its steps.

Before you start looking for jobs and completing online job applications, you'll need an updated version of your resume ready to upload.

You may also need a cover letter to apply for some jobs.

Ensure your resume includes your current contact information, a professional header, a complete work history (always start with the most recent experience), and any other certification or award.

Save your resume as name_surname.doc and add a professional photo to it.

Www.canva.com is a great source of free templates, although there are others a bit less equipped.

Cover letters are indeed becoming more and more outdated, but some companies still like them.

In case it is requested, make sure to keep it one page long, focus on your motivations and qualifications and try to personalize it.

A standard job interview can have from a minimum of one to potentially an indefinite number of steps.

This can vary according to the seniority of the role, niches, or responsibilities, but I'd say the average is 3 steps:

- After you submit your application, a Recruiter will review your CV and potential cover letter.

  With the help of an ATS (application tracking system) will determine whether your skills and experience match with the role requirements.

  If positive, the initial step is a *phone interview*.

  Many candidates commit the first mistake here because they underestimate it.

  On average, this screening call can last between 15 and 30 minutes but is already an official part of the selection process, and if you make a negative impression, you're not going to move forward.

  The scope is mainly to investigate further your resume, check if it is truthful, and spot potential gaps in your career path.

  One advice is to keep track of all your applications and, if you can, include a summary of each role and company you applied for; this will show commitment and motivation to the Interviewer.

  Also, you should feel confident!

You were invited to have an interview because the Manager thinks you could be a good fit.

- The second is the *behavioural examination*, better known as the *HR interview*.

  It can be video or in presence and takes around 1 hour; in both cases, it's held by the Recruiter or a representative from the Human Resources team.

  The main objective is to dig into your story, to get to know you better.

  Specifically, explore your soft skills, understand how your personality would fit the team structure and the company values, see your reaction to challenges and pressure, and check your ambitions and expectations (including salary).

  One advice is to be yourself, never pretend to oversell your abilities, or be too shy in showing vulnerabilities; we are all humans.

  Taking care of your outfit is also important.

  After, whether it's an email or a phone call to the Interviewers, reiterating your interest in the position and the company is always a good idea.

- The third step is the *technical interview*.

    Again, it can be video or in presence, it can last between 1 or 2 hours, and it's led by the Hiring Manager, often assisted by one of his / her team members.

    The goal is to examine your so-called hard skills, deep dive into your knowledge and competencies, and understand if you could do the job.

    Your process of reasoning and problem-solving is going to be tested.

    My advice is to remember that 99% of the time you'll be reporting to this Hiring Manager, therefore this step is the most important one, as, at the end of the process, his judgment is decisive. The HM may give you a tour of the office and even introduce you to other employees.

    The tour will provide you with an opportunity to meet your potential coworkers and assess the atmosphere of the office.

As anticipated before, there is no written rule about the number of steps you may face during the interview process.

In my experience, I met very determined HM and HR just as I met very confused ones.

It's all because they want to ensure they're hiring the best possible profile for that specific vacancy.

It's not easy!

Consequently, you can expect to have up to even 8 steps of the interview where you'll meet different representatives or members of the company, until potentially speaking with the CEO (most frequently with start-ups).

Two things I'd like to mention here are the psychometric tests and the group assessments.

The first ones, I must say, are becoming a bit obsolete, but still, you could have to deal with them.

They are preliminary written exercises that assist the Recruiters in predicting your personality traits and skills.

My personal opinion is that they aren't reliable because when applied to a selection process, they might reject candidates with potential that would only come out during a face-to-face or at maximum a video interview; but better to be prepared, online you can find many websites that can help you, for example a good one is https://www.jobtestprep.co.uk/.

The group assessments are instead a very valid option, the cons are that they require a big effort to be organized and indeed are not always mandatory.

Normally, big multinationals opt for this solution when they receive a considerable number of competitive candidates and decide to use group dynamics to observe and analyze potential day-to-day working activities.

One advice is to try to follow the circumstances, for example, do not pretend to stand up from the crowd by oppressing others but professionally defend your ideas.

Try to show courage without being aggressive.

The post-interview phase takes place in the days following the interview.

This is the time when the people you meet through the steps decide whether you are the best fit for the position, but is also the time when you can reflect on whether it is the right job for you or not.

If yes, a good strategy is to send a follow-up email or message (e.g. on LinkedIn).

By following up, you'll remind the Interviewers that you're a strong candidate for the job and reinforce that you're qualified and should be given serious consideration.

Most companies will respond with a yes or no within a week or two, although some companies take even longer to respond; some companies, unfortunately, do not respond unless you are going to receive a job offer.

The last step of a standard Recruitment process is indeed the offer, it is normally extended by the HR team after agreeing with the business on the salary and benefit perks.

Remember is a negotiation, hence you can try to get the best possible conditions; only pay attention when you pull too hard, and the rope breaks (we're going to talk about the salary negotiation more in detail later on in the book).

If you accept and sign the contract, finally complete the paperwork you will need to come on board as an employee of the company.

The forms include eligibility to work in the country, tax withholding, risk management policy, and other company-specific paperwork.

Usually, a dedicated onboarding team will reach out to you to provide support and guidance.

People and roles

Recruiter

noun [C] HR

UK / rɪˈkruːtər

A company or organization that is looking for new employees:

Corporate Recruiters *are visiting the university campus to interview final-year students.*

The Recruiter or Interviewer is the person leading the job interview.

Normally he has a Psychology or Human Resources background and is an expert in assessing people's skills and personality.

He can work autonomously as a freelance consultant, often specializing in proactive sourcing.

These workers are called *Head Hunters* because after receiving an assignment from a client, they hunt potential passive profiles from the job markets.

He can also be part of the Talent Acquisition team of a company or an organization; in this case, he answers the hiring needs of different teams and functions.

A Recruiter is a professional who works to match qualified individuals with specific open positions.

His job is to review a candidate's job experiences, negotiate salaries, and work with the Employers to make sure the fit works well for both parties.

It's also a Recruiter's job to stay on top of job trends, industry outlooks, and what qualities and skills companies are on the lookout for when hiring new employees.

Line Manager

noun [C] HR

UK / ˈlaɪn ˌmæn.ɪ.dʒər

The person who is directly responsible for managing someone else's work in a company or business is one level above that person.

In the selection process, he / she becomes the Hiring Manager | *Often those people on sick leave would just be left alone with little or no contact from their Line Manager.*

A Hiring Manager is a person who supervises the hiring process and is responsible for filling open job positions.

Alone do not work towards Recruitment, but have a team to lead and supervise.

The hiring Manager coordinates with the HR team during the interviewing process to make the final hiring decision after the necessary approvals.

He is normally a highly technical person who masters skills related to a company field.

A Line Manager is a business professional who ensures the daily operations of the organization they work for run smoothly.

His primary goal is to implement new business programs successfully and help the company achieve its organizational objectives; can work for a wide variety of industries, including food service, finance, retail media, etc.

HR Generalist

noun [C] HR

UK / eɪtʃ-ɑː ˈdʒɛnərəlɪst

A Human Resource (HR) Generalist is a professional who is responsible for making sure that employees follow all policies and procedures.

He is responsible for creating new onboarding plans and educating newly hired employees about their rights.

An employee who typically reports to an HR Manager or Director.

HR Generalist handles daily core HR functions, such as Recruitment, employee relations, compensation, and compliance.

HR Business Partner

noun [C] HR

UK / HR bíznəs pá:tnə

A Human Resources Business Partner, or HRBP, is an HR professional who can handle everything from hiring and benefits to compliance and employee relations.

The HR Business Partner direct his clients on how to best reduce employment-related risks.

His guidance covers the full range of HR issues that can happen on any given day: employee conflicts, compliance questions, worker classifications, HR policy, turnovers, and more.

Some HRBPs even have industry-specific knowledge and can help their HM hiring strategically; is a professional communicator who knows HR codes and guidelines and can help businesses find the root cause of employee challenges.

He usually has a degree in Human Resources in addition to extensive HR experience, which he gained by working in several industries and with companies that operate across multiple states.

Payroll Specialist

noun [C] (PERSON)

UK / peɪ.rəʊl speʃ.əl.ɪst/

Payroll specialists, also called Payroll Clerks, play a vital role in organizations by ensuring all employees are paid on time and in full.

Because a Payroll Specialist's job is to manage data related to employee pay, this professional may work as part of a Finance team and / or in the HR department.

He manages the implementation of the payments and benefits for each employee and the company as a whole.

Admin

noun [C] (PERSON)

UK / ˈæd.mɪn

Short for Administrator: a person who is in charge of the operation of a network of computers, a website, a group of computer users, etc., and can make changes to it | *Only Admins can add people to the group chat or change the name of the group.*

During the selection process, an Admin can be part of the Human Resources team and help with administrative tasks; help manage and prepare different documents, help employees with issues that arise, facilitate employee onboarding and training, and may even help with payroll:

e.g. posting a job opportunity online, scheduling the interviews with the candidate, reserving a room for a meeting together with booking the necessary equipment, or often supporting the onboarding activities by handling the background check, relocation documents, etc.

Candidate

noun [C] HR

UK /ˈkæn.dɪ.dət

A person who competes to get a job or elected position | *Three candidates standing in the selection.*

It is the person whose mix of skills, personality, experience, and attitude should match the needs of the vacancy.

Can be a passive or active candidate, depending on if he / she applied directly for the job or has been proposed to it.

An active candidate is an applicant who is in the middle of the recruiting process and is actively seeking a job.

He can be undergoing the screening procedure, getting ready for an interview, or competing against another candidate.

A passive job candidate is a professional who isn't actively looking for a new job, but is open to the right opportunity.

Normally, he is a professional currently working in other companies, startups, or organizations; this means that he is probably not available immediately.

Preparation before the interviews

An interview is an opportunity for both you and the Employer to decide whether you are a good fit for the role.

Whether you are a student or a fresh graduate, or you have been out of the workforce, your job interview does not have to be an intimidating experience.

You don't need to memorize the answers but do take the time to consider how you'll respond.

The more you prepare, the more confident you'll feel during a job interview.

I'm going to split this chapter into three sections.

Preparation before the phone interview, preparation before the HR interview, and preparation before the technical interview:

- The first is surely the most underestimated step of the whole process.

   People often send their CVs randomly to dozens of job applications, even forgetting they applied.

   Then, when the Recruiter calls them without advanced notice, they are caught completely unprepared.

   Disastrous!

   As I've already anticipated before, this is a critical step because if you don't make a positive impression during this initial conversation, you're never going to meet any HM (remember they're the decision makers of who are going to be the hired candidates).

   It is fundamental to make some preparations.

   Firstly, track every role you apply for in an Excel file and write down the name of the company - sector - job title - and date of the application.

   Do some research, prepare some answers and questions, then you have to jot them down in a notebook, a post-it, or in a one-page document and stick to bullet points.

Quick tip, you certainly don't want to be reading your answers off like a script, that'll just make you sound inauthentic.

I know it's an effort, but looking for a job is a job in itself, the sooner you understand this, the more chances of getting hired you're going to have.

Also, when you receive the call at home, you may want to lock yourself in a room that's away from family, roommates, or pets; at work, book a conference room, find a coffee shop nearby, or settle for your car or a quiet side street to avoid annoying sounds.

During the call, you don't have to jump straight into business!

At least not if they aren't.

Feel free to ask them how their day's going, talk about the weather or your weekend, or try a conversation starter if it seems natural.

One of the biggest mistakes people make in phone interviews is not sounding energetic and excited enough.

Because the person can't see you, you have to work extra hard to show that you're enthusiastic about the role.

Don't forget to take notes during the call and at the end think of sending a thank-you message.

Last, if you can't do these hacks, and you still receive the call from the Recruiter, remember that you can gain some time.

Be smart, answer the phone, and politely ask to schedule the conversation for another moment so that you can make some preparations beforehand.

I bet no Recruiter will refuse it.

- The second is the one that requires the biggest preparation.

  The HR team is there to challenge you, to make you unveil your inner personality, and to understand if you can fit the company and the role.

  Since you'll be asked to answer competency-based and behavioural questions, it is a good strategy to draw up answers that can help you to show your reasoning, values, and in general all the so-called soft skills.

  For example: adaptability, problem-solving, leadership, critical thinking, teamwork and collaboration, time management, flexibility, empathy, listening, confidence, work ethic, reliability, emotional intelligence, creativity, communication, conflict resolution, and resilience.

  Of course, you can't predict exactly what question you will be asked; still, you can learn to express thoughts clearly, structure your sentences, pick the most adequate words, remain calm and confident, show motivation and interest, and be persuasive.

  Another piece of advice is to study the company and learn about its history, values, products, company vision, and strategy.

Nowadays, online you can easily access this information.

You can practice your communication skills by using online tutorials, talking to yourself in a mirror, or enlisting the help of a friend.

Continued practice may help you speak with more confidence.

Whether you go for a face-to-face or a video meeting, dress appropriately, the way you dress depends on the type of Employer you're applying to, so consider factors like their company culture and work environment.

Master your CV and cover letter, and be ready to explain in detail every single word you put into them.

If it's in person, plan and leave plenty of time for your journey.

Make sure you know which bus or train you need to take, and what time it leaves or where the nearest parking is.

Believe me, it's always better to arrive early and kill time in a nearby café until your interview rather than risk turning up late.

If it's on video, make sure to find a quiet place at home or wherever you are with a neutral background (avoid teenagers' posters, or I don't know the walls of a private political café).

- Last but not least, the technical interview.

    To be ready to face this examination, you better study the role in detail.

    Make sure you thoroughly review the job description and understand the responsibilities and qualifications required for the position.

    Understand what tools and technology they use, research the plus and minus of them, if you can, check their functioning and think of potential improvements; study the main features, what they would expect from you, and how your knowledge can be beneficial for them.

    Maybe you could consider reviewing some university books to refresh your theoretical education.

    Please bring examples, the more specific and concrete you can be the better.

    Another astute thing you can do is search the HM online, for example on LinkedIn; try to understand what kind of career path they had, their expertise, and their current projects, and use them in your favour to support your argumentation and to show a potential match.

    Hiring Managers love to see passion for the job or the industry, they always give value to engagement rather than mere execution of a task.

If you want to ace it, consider bringing samples of your work, projects, models, or anything else that would concretely support your verbal exposition.

Behavioural vs technical examination

Behavioural interviewing is a technique used to question a job candidate about his / her experiences.

It's based on the premise that past performance is an excellent predictor of future behaviour.

The Society for Human Resource Management (SHRM) suggests using this method to learn about an applicant's specific skills, abilities, behaviours, and knowledge.

The questions highlight verifiable evidence about previous actions in the workplace.

Recruiters often use the STAR method during these examinations.

It is an interview approach that gives you a straightforward format you can use to tell a story by laying out the situation, task, action, and result:

- *Situation* - Set the scene and give the necessary details of your example;
- *Task* - Describe what your responsibility was in that situation;
- *Action* - Explain exactly what steps you took to address it;
- *Result* - Share what outcomes your actions achieved;

Inevitably, you're now wondering ok, but how am I going to be prepared for this step?

Number one, prepare a few stories based on the job description.

Read it carefully and make a list of top skills or qualifications it calls for, then think of a story that demonstrates your ability in each area.

Number two, practice your storytelling (the vivid description of ideas, beliefs, personal experiences, and life lessons through stories or narratives that evoke powerful emotions and insights), either by yourself or with a friend.

Number three, wrap up your answers with a conclusion: make sure to conclude your story with a nice summary so that the Interviewer knows what they were supposed to learn from it.

And last, keep your answers under two minutes.

The tendency is to rush your speech, especially if you're sensitive to the tension and anxiety of the moment, but the most important thing is to be concrete and concise.

As someone used to say, less is more.

A *technical examination,* instead, is an evaluation of an individual's ability to perform a specific task or job.

These assessments are commonly used in the hiring process to identify candidates with the necessary skills and knowledge to be successful in a role.

It is more common for Employers recruiting for science, technology, engineering, or mathematics (STEM).

Companies that incorporate technical assessments into their hiring processes can identify top talent and make well-educated hiring choices.

For example, they can:

- Produce numerical values that can help companies compare candidates (this is useful if many candidates have similar skills, experiences, or qualifications);
- Enhance individual experience; they give each candidate the chance to show their capabilities;
- Enable candidates to ask more specific questions about the role and understand its nuances;

Typically, this step is to analyse and observe the problem-solving attitude.

Precisely, Employers check how a candidate gathers information from various sources, uses critical thinking to evaluate information, makes decisions that help the business, and communicates his findings or recommendations to team members.

There may be multiple rounds of onsite interviews with different teams.

Make sure to clarify the format and ask with whom you will be interviewing ahead of time.

If you want to impress them, offer multiple approaches to the problems, but if you make a mistake, try not to let it throw you off guard.

The questions are designed to challenge the very brightest of us; demonstrate instead an eagerness to learn by asking the Interviewer questions.

ATS & virtual interviews

ATS is the acronym for *Application Tracking System*.

It is a software application that enables the electronic handling of Recruitment and hiring needs.

An ATS can be implemented or accessed online at enterprise or small-business levels, depending on the needs of the organization; free and open-source ATS software is also available.

It is typically very similar to customer relationship management (CRM) systems but is designed for Recruitment tracking purposes.

In many cases, they filter applications automatically based on given criteria such as keywords, skills, former Employers, years of experience and schools attended.

This practice of application filtering has caused many to adopt resume optimization techniques similar to those used in search engine optimization

(SEO) when creating and formatting their curriculum vitae.

Indeed, the most effective strategy you can apply not to be blocked by them, is to read the job description and before applying, add the most used keywords to your CV.

In this way, you increase the chances of beating the machine.

Virtual interviews are job interviews that don't take place in person.

Typically, Interviewers use video conferencing tools to see and speak with remote candidates.

According to LinkedIn, more than 65% of professionals agree that the impression you make online is just as important as the one you make in person.

They have become integral to many hiring processes; they can be conducted remotely and asynchronously, save time and money, are convenient for Recruiters and candidates, improve candidate experience, and reduce unconscious bias in hiring.

Some companies use specialized online interview platforms, while others take place via video call software like Zoom, Skype, or Microsoft Teams.

Asynchronous virtual interview platforms mimic a traditional interview structure but allow candidates to complete them on the device and at the time of their choice.

The most famous is Hire Vue.

Virtual interviews can last anywhere from 15 minutes to over an hour, depending on where in the process the candidate is, how many Interviewers there are, and what is being assessed.

Just like face-to-face.

The biggest difference is that while Recruiters and Hiring Managers oversee every Recruitment process via virtual interview, in some cases, artificial intelligence (AI) can be integrated into the process to increase efficiency and reduce human bias and error.

AI-powered virtual interviews have speed in their favour.

Instead of a person having to sit down with each candidate and conduct the interview themselves, the AI platform can guide the candidate through each question and record their responses.

It then reviews these responses and scores candidates based on a framework chosen by the hiring company.

I believe more in the human touch of the Recruiters, but in the end, it is always about money and cost-saving plans.

Some advice for candidates:

- Ask in advance which tool to use
- Ask about the process
- Check your internet connection
- Pick a neutral spot in your home
- Be ready to complete some tests
- Agree on the next steps

The 101 questions

Finally, the most awaited chapter of the book, the questions.

Below are the 101 most frequently asked questions of any given selection process and how to answer them.

I grouped them according to different steps and topic areas.

a. Kick-off:

Lasting approximately two to five minutes, you are meeting the Interviewers and being escorted to the interview room.

You must start strong, offer a firm handshake, stand confidently, and make good eye contact.

1. Tell me about yourself.

It's a standard ice-breaking question that helps to make the candidate feel more relaxed.

I always recommend doing a quick breathing exercise before getting in the interviewing room, then start to tell your story, focusing on relevant accomplishments and events.

For example, graduation and studies, professional certifications, work experience (including student or volunteering activities) but also sports achievements, or passions and hobbies.

Important is to follow a chronological order;

2. Walk me through your resume.

Same as above, it belongs to the ice-breaking questions.

A good practice is to print out a few copies of your CV, hand them over to your Interviewers, and hold one for you to guide you through the conversation.

Remember not to rush your speech and make pauses; avoid too many details if are not asked;

3. What did you study and why?

The Interviewers want to understand if your study path was a conscious and autonomous choice or if it was a forced decision by external factors (e.g. family business / expectations).

Important is to explain how you arrived at the decision and possibly if you have any happy moments or regrets;

4. **Have you ever done an internship or a volunteering activity during your students' years?**

   This question is quite common for students or fresh graduates; since they don't have any official working experience yet, the Recruiter tries to predict the potential behaviour and workplace adaptation.

   Advice: even a Boy Scout experience could spotlight your potential;

5. Why haven't you continued your studies?

For highly specialized roles or public competitions, it is important to have completed a full cycle of studies, actually, sometimes it is even mandatory to be able to participate in the selection process.

In general, it happens quite often that candidates prefer to start working before their completion, in these cases, it is important to properly explain the reason for leaving the studies (e.g. help the family to pay the bills).

Advice: never show that the real reason was lack of motivation or boredom;

6. What are your passions?

Recruiters love to ask this question for a full picture of your profile.

It is simple but very effective in understanding candidates' nuances.

Ideally, your passions should be linked to your job or preferably should highlight your positive traits.

For example, painting can show creativity, gardening patience, pet training emotional intelligence, bricolage manual skills, etc.;

7. What do you normally do in your free time?

Same as above, the key here is to show them that you invest your free time into something positive and useful.

Even being part of a sports team is seen as an advantage because it can help you grow collaboration and leadership skills.

To avoid are answers like "I love to sleep until late", "I normally watch television and do zapping all the time", or "I sit in a pub every evening";

8. Do you have any certification?

Don't forget to mention them, they are a plus to your profile and can differentiate you from other candidates.

Also, they show your commitment to developing your skills and willingness to grow, they can be technical certificates (e.g. PMI-project management, AutoCAD, QC-control, etc.) or related to your soft skills (e.g. first aid, dog training, gym personal training, etc.);

9. How would you describe yourself?

The most important thing is to show that you're a balanced person, in the sense that you know yourself, your capacities, and your limits.

Don't restrict the answer to the professional sphere, but bring examples from outside the workplace, and try to show self-confidence without turning it into arrogance.

For example, talk about your sports sphere, the reading circle you frequent, or I know of your passion for animals;

10. How do others describe you?

It's normally asked in sequence after the question above because the Recruiter would like to understand if you have been honest before and whether your friends and family confirm your view of yourself or not.

It's important to be self-conscious of who we are and how we're perceived by others;

11. How did you hear about this position?

It is a standard question asked to understand if you have any connections inside the company or if you have been following their communications and updates.

It could also be useful for the HR team to analyse which job advertisement platform works better;

12. Why did you apply for this role?

This is quite important to address the interview in the right way.

HM and Recruiters are looking for motivated people, engaged with the brand, and people who will represent the company, hence the best way to answer here is by showing commitment.

For example, you like the company's sustainable view, or you are interested in their latest software release, or maybe you're a top customer of their best-selling product.

Curiosity is also very welcome;

13. Describe a typical work week.

A discursive response where you ideally present in chronological order your main tasks and responsibilities would be the best, but also a structured list of actions could work.

The more details and examples you can give, the better, but pay attention not to exaggerate.

Advice: look at the Interviewers, if they're following you or not, and from their facial expressions try to recognize if you can continue or if is the case to cut it short;

14. What were the main responsibilities and tasks of your last role?

Before going to the interview, write down a list of all tasks and responsibilities of your last and previous role (at least).

Do not take some for granted and remember to explain them properly, what is obvious to you could not be to the listeners.

Emphasize the ones that can showcase your abilities and positive traits, and avoid prolonging the boring / non-relevant ones (e.g. administrative and repetitive tasks);

15. Why would you like to work for us?

It's one of the most common questions that a Recruiter will ask during the job interview, and still, most candidates continue to struggle.

In my decade of experience, I observed different strategies applied: the praise for the company, the ambitious individualism, the reverse answer, or even the disinterested act.

As mentioned above, it is normally asked at the beginning of the interview and is used to understand your motivations. It is preferred to avoid narcissistic answers like "I'm looking for a salary increase" or "I want to be promoted" but instead try to underline positive attractive factors like "I read great reviews about you as an Employer of choice" or "I would like to learn how you became a big player in your industry" etc.;

b. Behavioural:

Behavioural-based interview questions are perhaps some of the most challenging questions you'll ever encounter in an interview.

They are based on the theory that past experiences are a better indicator of future behaviour rather than hypothetical situations.

In place of an Employer asking you how you would handle certain situations, they will ask you how you handled situations.

16. Can you give me an example of a situation where you managed a complex case?

For all behavioural questions, a good strategy is to use the STAR method in the answer (Situation-Task-Action-Result).

For example, if you're a technical expert you could give an example of a situation where you received an alert and had to react quickly; if you're a People Manager you could think of sharing an example of a time when you dealt with internal escalations. The key is to show composure in front of unexpected criticalities;

17. Describe a situation where you had to explain a complex concept to a coworker or client.

Illustrate how you explained the concept step by step, used a procedural method, avoided technicalities, and added details.

Remark the simple words picked and the easily understandable examples shown to help grasp the concept.

It is valuable to show that you are patient and that repeating things several times is not an issue.

Clarity of exposition is also observed;

18. How do you approach a situation where you don't have all the answers?

What they would like to see here is your reaction to uncertainty.

Especially in executive positions, you're called to make difficult decisions where it is unrealistic or highly improbable to have all the answers but still, you must show boldness.

The risk is to exaggerate, remember that balance is pivotal.

My advice is to analyse all aspects out loud, and reason with them;

19. What would you do if you received an escalation?

Escalations can be for technical issues or for employees' behaviours (especially if you manage a team, you would receive it from other stakeholders).

Again, highly appreciated are the people who remain calm and don't lose objectivity.

Demonstrate a can-do attitude toward solving the problem / conflict;

20. Can you provide an example of when you showed initiative?

Proactivity is everything.

Passive people who wait for problems to happen and react are not well seen in the current job market.

It doesn't have to be the solution or the idea of the century, but it is necessary to prove your out-of-the-box thinking.

For example, tell of that time you saw a gap in the process, and you suggested an implementation or a time when you proposed an unsatisfied client a good deal, etc.;

21. Can you describe a situation where you didn't get along with a colleague?

Normally, you should never have problems with your colleagues.

Companies don't like to hire people that could break the team's serenity and equilibrium.

But of course, you may disagree with someone, or you may have a very different personality that will never make you good friends with a deskmate.

In these cases, it is appreciated to show that you keep your misunderstanding outside the workplace, and even though you think negatively of someone, you're able to still cooperate with them for the sake of closing the project;

22. How would you react to a complaint?

Complaints are part of the business game. The more you manage to accept and absorb them constructively, the better for you and your career progression.

It is utopian to think that you can perpetually make everyone happy, you have to consider that there will always be someone that will have different opinions and ideas from yours.

In these cases, it is imperative to not over-react and to address complaints properly;

23. Can you describe a time when your work was criticized?

Same as above, criticisms, if motivated, are essential to your growth!

To avoid here is bringing examples where you went mad because you thought they were unjustified or because you felt that your work and efforts went wasted etc.

Don't forget that even the most brilliant minds were often criticized, but what differentiated them from the average was how they reacted;

24. When you're working on multiple projects, how do you keep yourself organized?

We all have different methods, what would be logical and easy for me could not be for you; plus, multitasking is often overrated.

Nowadays, we operate in a highly connected world and this can have an impact on our daily jobs because it could mean more things to do or take care of.

I'm personally sensitive about this topic because it is very easy to get stressed and go into burnout.

In my opinion, the best thing you could do is show that you have a method, and you follow a logical order in doing multiple things but don't be afraid of showing your limits.

Knowing when to ask for help is a strong skill;

25. Tell me about a creative solution you have designed to address a work issue.

Creativity is another highly desired skill, but instead of multitasking, it can set you free.

Jobs that allow you to use your imagination, even if it's only for improving a procedure, are for me the best.

Imagine doing the same thing over and over again without having the possibility to even challenge your boss about its vulnerabilities, would be terrible, right?

So, you can in reality turn this question in your favour, after answering with your examples, ask the same question to the Interviewers.

It'll help you to better understand if this is the right role for you;

26. Describe when you had to think outside the box to solve a problem.

This question could potentially highlight two skills, creativity and problem-solving.

If you manage to mix both in your answer, you win.

Remember, every company big or small has problems, but people with the gift of solving them are scarce.

Thus, don't think of an example that could solve human history but of a good and solid case when you had an intuition that helped you and your team to overcome a threat or when your intuition helped to move on from being stuck.

Humility and simplicity are highly appreciated skills;

c. Culture fit:

Company culture refers to the shared values, beliefs, attitudes, and behaviours that shape the overall personality and character of an organization.

It is the sum of all the collective experiences, interactions, and relationships that occur within the workplace, including how employees communicate with each other, how they work together, and how they perceive their work environment.

27. Describe your work ethic.

Work ethic means a series of behaviours and moral norms to be held to ensure a positive working environment.

For example: reliability, dedication, discipline, productivity, cooperation, integrity, responsibility, and professionalism.

But also means keeping your interactions professional to show your respect for colleagues.

Hiring Managers ask this question because employees with strong work ethics are highly motivated and produce consistently high-quality results;

28. Describe your ideal company culture.

Interviewers would like to understand how well you fit the organization's culture.

Do some preparation before the interview and check the company's mission, objectives, strategies, and how management communicates these with staff members; then explain how you can contribute to that;

29. Do you prefer working independently or in a team?

Of course, it depends on the nature of the role, sometimes there are opportunities for remote people to be part of the so-called IT Hubs where a high grade of independence and self-discipline are needed; but typically, the answer should aim to reiterate your teamwork approach.

Companies are made of people, maybe people who already found team harmony, and they don't want to ruin that by adding employees with individualistic or selfish traits;

30. What is a time you disagreed with a decision that was made at work?

We all had disagreements with someone once in a lifetime, there is no shame in sharing it.

But inevitably, if it becomes a habit, it is a problem.

When bringing your example, make sure to explain why you disagreed and what steps you took to find a resolution.

It's great to defend our opinions and ideas, but we should also be capable of finding compromises and making a step back if needed;

31. **Tell me about a time you made a mistake.**

"The worst mistake is to not make any"

Should I say more? I think it is clear by now that my belief is we are all humans, and as such, we're subject to mistakes.

No one is perfect, nor will ever be (not even your Recruiter).

Therefore, don't be afraid of talking about mistakes, the only necessary thing is to include what you learned from them and how you tried to avoid their repetition the subsequent time;

32. What type of work environment do you prefer?

You can be honest in your answer because the work environment is where normally we spend one-third of our life.

Some examples are: positive, flexible, understanding, respectful, productive, trustful, diversified, supportive, promote collaboration, foster growth, and with a good sense of humour which never hurts;

33. How do you like to be managed?

Another question that can be knotty but is very appreciated by Hiring Managers.

On average, we like autonomous people who require little guidance and can perform from day one, but the reality is different.

Especially at the beginning, new joiners, regardless of seniority, need mentorship and guidance, this is why companies look for people who are good listeners, accept feedback, observe, and put into practice fearless of making mistakes.

Important is to accept the hierarchy and respect your superiors;

34. What is your teaching philosophy?

Many Employers focus on hiring employees with great teaching philosophy and teaching skills, as it improves the reputation of their organization.

Teaching is a highly requested skill in current People Managers; often you hire candidates with potential but to be refined on the job, and therefore it is desired to have leaders with methods who act as role models and guide them;

35. What does customer service mean to you?

At this historical moment, it doesn't matter the nature and sector of your business, you have to take care of your customers.

Even the executive management has to.

Customer service means an approach that is personalized, empathetic, competent, proactive, attentive, resourcefulness, helpful, solution-oriented, patient, and listening.

Don't forget, the client is always right;

36. How do you make a client happy?

This question is on the edge of being part of the tricky group, but I preferred to include it here because it could be another occasion to show your positive values.

For example: honesty, politeness, respect, advisory, reliability, hard work, etc.

We have to make the client happy is a sentence you'll often hear, but it is necessary to set some limits: if you notice that a client is trying to bring the conversation into bribery, or corruption or if you feel seriously disrespected, immediately stop and report it to your Manager or flag it to the Compliance team;

37. What would you do if you saw a coworker doing something dishonest?

If he / she is your direct report clearly, you'd want to have a private meeting to discuss what happened and then take appropriate disciplinary actions, but if you're peers, maybe even friends, it is more difficult.

In these cases, it is expected that you follow the company guidelines: typically disclose it to your Line Manager or Compliance team or raise an HR ticket.

Never hide it or keep it under your desk;

38. What is your approach to maintaining work-life balance?

Work-life balance is a trendy topic in the modern job market.

In Recruitment, we swing between new generations who are quite lazy and consider work almost as a hobby and old-school Managers who consider work the primary reason for living.

The truth is always in the middle, consider explaining that your private life is essential for your mental health, which has an impact on your job, but be ready to work extra time if a tight delivery deadline is approaching (obviously the exceptions don't have to become the rule);

39. Would you accept a bribe?

This question is on the edge of the embarrassing group you will find later, but I prefer to think of companies in good faith.

It could investigate your reaction to illegal instances that unfortunately in some sectors (sales predominantly) might happen.

The imperative is to show your integrity and even if it means losing a big deal, we should accept never illegal compromises;

d. Leadership:

Recruiters look for specific core skills in applicants that help retain them as company assets in the form of potential future leaders.

Leadership skills are a blend of essential strategic management and people skills that make candidates stand out and gain an edge over their peers at company interviews for senior positions.

The ideal candidate impresses Interviewers with their poise, ability to draw references from real-life experiences, and collaborative qualities.

40. What are your main strengths and your main weaknesses?

This common question is helpful for Interviewers to understand your personality and working style.

Everybody has both strengths and weaknesses.

Answering it right would help you to provide a context example of how you use your strengths to shine and how you work to improve any weaknesses relevant to the role.

For your strengths, be confident; mention one or two top strengths, and provide examples of how you've used them in the workplace.

If you can back this up with measurable results, even better.

For the weaknesses, the key is to pair self-awareness with an action and a result.

Explaining that you are aware of a particular weakness and have taken steps to improve is a sign of maturity and drive that is attractive to Employers;

41. What is your leadership style?

This question extends beyond managerial roles, as Hiring Managers also look out for leadership capabilities in candidates.

Describe good management, doesn't have to be inside the workplace, maybe at school, you led a group of students for homework, or in your sports team, you once were the captain.

Some common and appreciated leadership styles are leading by example, leading by facilitating communication, or leading by delegating and making others better;

42. What is your management style?

Essentially, you could do micro or macro-management.

The optimal would be to be able to adopt and switch both styles according to needs.

For example, if you have new joiners would be wise to start with micro-management, stay closer to them to supervise their work and correct it in case of need; but if you have senior employees, they would most probably want to take advantage of more trust and autonomy of the macro-management style;

43. How do you prioritize your work?

The Interviewer may ask you this question to gain insight into how you manage your time and organize your workload.

Important is to have a method.

Describe how you schedule your day, shift priorities, delegate if needed, and meet deadlines; try to focus on bringing real-life examples without forgetting about the work-life balance (being work-alcoholic is wrong);

44. Define success.

Success is a term that means different things to different people.

For some, it may mean reaching a certain level of financial stability and career progression; in contrast, for others, success may mean having a fulfilling personal life or positively impacting the world.

Success is subjective, and there is no one-size-fits-all answer; only make sure not to sound too egocentric;

45. Define failure.

We all experience failure, but only some people know how to learn from it to be more successful in the future.

In a "winning-is-everything" society you might be nervous about sharing a time you failed, but on the opposite, showing that we're capable of feeling emotions is a great skill.

What Interviewers want to listen to are people who learn from mistakes, take out the positive, and accept them constructively;

46. How do you deal with pressure?

Undoubtedly, pressure isn't for everyone.

In my opinion, a work environment where working under pressure is a must-have skill is a toxic one.

Therefore, turn this question in your favour and use it to understand the real nature of the workplace.

The ideal way to deal with pressure should be to not panic during workload peak moments and try to maintain consistent delivery standards;

47. How do you cope with stress?

Usually, absorbing and channelling stress is very much needed in the modern labour market.

Hence, you may want to sound like a professional who manages to control it preserving the standards of your performance but same as above, pay attention to how they ask it and what kind of answer the Interviewers expect because it can be another indicator of a potentially toxic workplace;

48. Are you a risk-taker?

Taking calculated risks is a required skill of today's leaders.

Risks are what make companies grow, knowing how to recognize opportunities and make reasoned hazards is needed, especially when you operate in uncertainty.

Beyond doubt, though, you don't want to be labelled as a gambler, as always find balance in your answer;

49. Give an example of how you've motivated others.

A huge part of success is being capable of motivating others.

For example, first and foremost, how do you motivate others without listening to them? Secondly, try to ask the right questions!

Third, set smart goals (specific, measurable, achievable, relevant, and time-bound), provide support, adapt your management style, and last but not least live your values by acting as a role model;

50. What strategies do you use to make decisions?

Companies, private or public, want to have people comfortable and confident in making decisions, but strong decision-makers are scarce.

Essential to highlight is the process of coming to a decision.

For example, gather relevant information, weigh pros and cons, identify and scan alternatives, forecast consequences, take actions, and review the results;

e. Career aspirations:

Career aspirations are long-term hopes and ambitions.

People develop them based on their personal experiences, including talents, values, lifestyle, and more.

For the career aspirations question, Interviewers especially want to know that you have put thoughts into your future career and mapped out specific goals to manifest your aspirations.

51. Where do you see yourself in the next 3 years?

It's not a personal question, so quell any desire to talk about your dreams to travel, have a family, or become a professional climber.

The Interviewer wants to identify your professional goals, specifically for the near future.

Prove to be realistic and to have a balanced career approach, it's preferable to hire people who can wait for the right time to come when working toward achieving a promotion;

52. Where do you see yourself in the next 10 years?

It's a long-term question, aimed at understanding your ultimate ambitions and aspirations.

To impress Interviewers, make your answer related to the job and the company you're interviewing for.

Explain that you want to grow in the role and take on more responsibilities as time progresses, companies look for people to invest in them and build long-term plans;

53. Provide an example of a goal you reached and tell us how you achieved it.

The example doesn't necessarily have to be related to your working life, what is meaningful is the process of goal setting.

Some tips: brainstorm, ask yourself questions (follow the rule of the 5W: why, what, when, who, and where), write it down, make a plan, take action, be accountable, reflect, and adjust.

Highly valued are achievements from sports or student associations;

54. What did you do in the last year to expand your knowledge?

Life-long learning is a doctrine companies follow.

Not only do they want to hire professionals with the potential to be expanded and attained, but they search for candidates with the right attitude; the need to learn new things, the curiosity for different points of view, and the determination to explore have become must-have skills.

Also, contamination (in the sense of taking from multiple disciplines in pursuance of improving something) is a trendy tendency;

55. What is your biggest ambition?

If your goals inspire you to work hard, you may be more likely to create good work for the company instead of someone who uses their Manager's instruction as their motivation.

In general, your biggest ambition should be becoming the best version of yourself, or at least trying to get the closest to it.

Once again, avoid unrealistic or self-centred answers like "I dream of becoming company CEO in 5 years";

56. What motivates you?

There is no right or wrong here, we all have different motivators; and to be honest, diversity is the beauty of life.

Whatever you say about your motivation, you need to back it up with examples.

They can be from your studies, work experience, or extracurricular activities, and they should relate to the skills and aptitudes required for the job you're competing for (or at most with the ambitions listed before);

57. What scares you?

Again, don't be afraid of sharing your weaknesses.

The only recommendation is, whatever you say, make certain to point out that you're conscious of them and that you're working on overcoming them.

Possibly try to bring examples pertinent to work;

58. What is your greatest accomplishment?

To pick the right answer, consider your background as well as the job description of the role you're interviewing for.

The best answer will show the Hiring Manager that your greatest accomplishment is both impressive and relevant to their team's needs.

Abilities to show could be determination, resilience, and adaptability (even better with a problem-solving temperament);

59. What is your biggest regret?

This question can cause candidates to stumble, vital is to explain why you consider it your biggest regret.

Same as talking about fears, we all have regrets; describe honestly how you handled them, remember to show that you learned something valuable from them and, didn't make the same mistake twice;

60. What are you looking for in a new position?

This question could potentially be considered a trap, but I decided to put it in this group because you can use it to reiterate and reinforce your motivations.

If possible, bring the focus back to the company as you're wrapping up your response but avoid talking about financial wishes or promotion urgencies (give time to time);

61. What is your dream job?

The Interviewers ask this type of question to understand your passion, motivation, and values as an employee.

However, they would also like to know whether you're satisfied with the job position if you got the job offer; also, you can include what kind of work environment and company culture you would prefer to work in and how it will positively impact you;

f. Technical skills:

Technical interviews are an opportunity for a potential Employer to learn about your technical knowledge, including the tools you use and the practical skills you possess.

Technical questions tend to be more targeted than behavioural interview questions, so Interviewers can understand the extent of what you know, your ability to solve problems and think critically, and how prepared you are to begin the role should you get an offer.

62. What software tools do you have experience with?

Don't think this question is only for developers or IT people in general, in the modern labour market, technology plays a relevant role in basically every job.

It's important to specify what level of experience you have with each tool, starting from the one you use the most.

Advice for you, always stay up to date with the latest sector tech releases and features;

63. How do your skills align with this role?

Very important question! Aligning your skills with the job description is an art.

Mention the specific skills and qualifications from the job description that align with your background, and explain how these will help you excel in the role.

Also, share a brief anecdote or example of how you've successfully used similar competencies in the past;

64. How quickly do you adapt to new technology?

As stated above, staying up to date with new technologies is not only recommended, but is often expected by the Employer.

Not everyone though is a tech-savvy person, what is being considered is the learning process.

The 4-don'ts rule: don't be afraid of trying new tools or experimenting with different systems, don't be shy in asking questions, don't forget to take notes, and don't mess it up (as a general rule it is better to adopt new technology slowly);

65. How would you use this tool / platform?

The Hiring Manager wants to observe your thinking and acting process; it isn't indispensable to master the tool but is rather important to show how you'd learn to use it. Start with the documentation, play around with it, watch video tutorials, practice, join online communities, and if needed ask for help;

66. Can you explain the steps you take to troubleshoot a technical problem?

If calling IT support is not an option, you should be able to fix the issue yourself or at least minimize the damage.

Again, focus your answer on listing the steps you'd take and put emphasis on the problem-solving approach: identify the root cause, establish a theory, test the theory, establish a plan, verify its functionality, and document the solution.

Advice: keep it simple;

67. What are some limitations of your favourite software tools?

What is tested here is your attitude toward out-of-the-box thinking.

Be critical but keep a balance: open your answer by asking questions, get inspiration, accept contamination, and take some risks (reasonable risks preferably).

Don't criticize too much the other tools, remember to remain neutral;

g. Tricky:

During a job interview, your Interviewer may ask you questions that require more thoughtful answers.

Even if interview questions can vary widely between industries, there are several tough questions Employers commonly ask to learn more about you as a candidate and assess your skills.

68. What do you expect from the job?

A lot of times candidates have a different picture in mind than what is the reality of the company.

It is essential to keep all your answers optimistic during an interview; you should always reflect on positive experiences and the things you liked most about your previous / future positions, and avoid discussing areas of stress or concern.

Also, do your homework, study the job description, and use your own words to explain the job duties based on the job description;

69. What are the last 5 positions you applied for?

This is one of the trickiest job interview questions ever, the Recruiter is testing your real motivation for the role and company.

Typical scenarios: if you don't remember the last 5 positions you applied for is a sign of scarce professionalism because you probably sent your CV randomly; if you remember the last 5 positions you applied for, but they are completely different from one another it means that you are just looking for a job not interested to work for that company or sector.

The best answer is to either list 5 positions in the same industry sector or 5 positions with the same job title, in this way, you demonstrate decision and motivation;

70. Why should we hire you?

What makes it so tough is that it's a very open-ended question, and can be answered in several different ways.

You can, for example, go over your resume and explain how your work experience makes you a great fit for the role, or you can talk about how you possess certain skills that make you stand out from other candidates.

Enthusiasm is a critical component of the final decision of whom to hire;

71. Why did you change jobs?

If they ask in the plural, it is because they probably spotted you have changed a bit too often; it is not a killer question per se but depending on how you answer it could be.

Companies want to hire candidates who marry their organizations, it is counterproductive to invest time and money in resources that will leave you soon.

My recommendation is to stay within the role for a minimum of 3–4 years before changing unless you have a very good reason; in that case, be ready to explain it (business acquisition or merger, company downturn or restructuring, professional development or family circumstances, etc.);

72. Are you applying for other jobs?

The Interviewer is looking for answers to a few points when asking this question.

The company wants to know what kind of timeline is present before you are scooped up by another organization; how selective you are with your job applications; the types of roles that interest you; hear that they are your top choice;

73. Have you ever had an interview with us?

Due to company policy, on average, you can't repeat a job interview if you were rejected less than 6 months ago (this is because it is supposed that to acquire new skills relevant to the role, it'd take longer).

Also, the Recruiter is trying to understand if you have any connection inside the company which would help them capture additional references;

74. What don't you like about your current or ex-company?

We have a saying in Italy "Never spit on the plate where you have eaten", it applies very well here, right?

Your response should be focused on balancing your feelings toward your previous Employer and how this new position can help you get to where you want to be in your career.

Make a list of the incompatible aspects of your last job but don't let frustration drive it;

75. Describe your best / worst boss.

Together with question number 69, it's undoubtedly in the top 3 of the trickiest questions ever.

We tend to complain about our superiors, but as you can probably imagine, you would not gain many points for such an answer in your job interview.

Focusing on the bad things is not an attitude Hiring Managers seek in their new employees; on the contrary, they prefer to hire people who see the good in others, and who can "praise" their bosses;

76. Describe your best / worst colleague.

Similar to the above, it is highly recommended to avoid complaints; instead of describing people, you can describe qualities.

For example, the best colleague would be flexible, reliable, communicative, punctual, and humble.

On the contrary, the worst colleague would be indecisive, unconfident, dishonest, passive, or even aggressive;

77. What can you bring to the company?

This interview question can be asked in various ways, however, it is easier to answer than you might think.

You just need to show why you'd be as good for the organization as they would be for you, by drawing connections between what you know about yourself and what you know about the Employer.

Neither underselling nor overselling yourself is the way to go with the answer here;

78. What will you miss about your last job?

The question is really about you, not your previous Employer.

When discussing what you'll miss about your last job, try to incorporate skills or challenges that you can apply to the position you're interviewing for, people that you grew to admire or became professionally close to and will stay in touch with you, can help show that you're not difficult to get along with.

Or maybe mention the positive office's culture etc.;

79. We see a gap in your resume, could you tell us what happened?

It's not the end of the world, but be sure to have a valid reason for absence from work for long periods.

You may have taken it for raising children, taking care of a sick or old family member, going back to school, or even travelling the world; these are good "excuses".

Avoid instead justifications like "I didn't know what to do" or "After terminating my last contract, I waited for someone to call me again";

80. Can you explain why you changed your career path?

I think you should address the question personally with one or two clear reasons.

You can avoid badmouthing your current job, Employer, or industry, and instead, focus on what you hope to gain in your next career path.

You can talk about how it's more in line with what you're passionate about, how you feel it could be a better industry for future growth and job security or even your values;

81. What other companies are you interviewing with?

It's important to note that it's completely acceptable and even expected for candidates to explore opportunities with multiple companies.

So, while they want to benchmark your interest, they also recognize that you're actively exploring your options to find the best fit.

Choose to give a summary of the types of companies (or industries) you're exploring, emphasizing the alignment between your skills, experience, and their respective roles;

82. What makes you unique?

Avoid two things when answering this question, generic phrases like "I'm a hard worker" and egocentric phrases like "I'm the best in my role".

On the contrary, help them determine how you stand out from other candidates: they want to know what specific qualities, skills, or experiences you possess that will bring success to the position they are trying to fill;

83. What should I know that's not on your resume?

Candidates are often thrown off guard by the question.

Instead, try to use it in your favour to highlight something special like sharing an interesting personal project or hobby that you're passionate about, an impactful volunteering experience, a unique training or certifications, or a recognition or awards you have won;

84. What do you think we could do better or differently?

It's a tricky question, Hiring Managers love to ask to interrogate your tact and communication style.

The only way you're going to be able to put together a good answer is if you research the company in advance; then use what you learned to identify specific aspects you admire and others you'd suggest changing (maybe consider the company values);

85. Have you ever been fired?

Everything in life is an experience, eventually also being fired; as long as you learn from it, and don't repeat the same mistake.

But in an interview, you have to provide explanations.

For example, "I was young and irresponsible", "It just wasn't the right field for me", "I have never been technically fired, but they terminated my contract once" etc.;

86. Do you prefer hard work or smart work?

While working hard and working smart are quite different approaches, ideally, you could find a balance between the two.

Hard work and smart work can go hand in hand.

While hard work requires dedicated effort, smart work demands advanced planning and innovative thinking; combining both types of work increases productivity and efficiency.

Your answer should be both;

87. Tell me something you would have done differently at work.

This is very close to the question asked about your past mistakes.

Make sure you carefully calibrate your answer to help your Employer understand that you always hope to learn from your mistakes.

In addition, avoid saying you have too many regrets, the risk is being labelled as a weak candidate;

88. What did you like least about your last position?

Another difficult question to navigate in a job interview.

Once more, the key is to stay positive, focus on the question, and turn the conversation back to your strengths.

It's important not to talk badly about your previous boss, colleagues, or company in general because it could come back to haunt you later on;

89. When could you start?

Although it may seem a straightforward question, it could trip you.

Experienced Recruiters are capable of spotting little signs not visible to a casual observer.

For example, you might wave because you are not sure of your interest in the position, you might want to gain time because you have other offers on the table, or you might be in desperate need of a job because you only got rejections recently.

On top of this, be prepared to give a date or commit to a time that you can respect as a start date;

h. Closing:

Closing an interview is important because it allows you to express more interest in the position, assess how well you did in the interview, and invite future contact from the Interviewer or Hiring Manager.

Finishing on a strong note is vital in increasing your chances of receiving an offer.

90. Do you have any references?

A reference is a statement written by someone who knows you and which describes your character and abilities.

When you apply for a job, an Employer might ask for references.

It's usually best to avoid using family members who may not have as much familiarity with your academic and professional experience and most importantly could have bias.

Warning: don't lie, serious Recruiters can verify their authenticity;

91. What would be your salary expectation?

There are lots of reasons why you may not want to answer questions about salary directly.

Nevertheless, Interviewers want to be sure they can afford you, and it's in their best interest not to waste their time (or yours!).

Consider giving a range, that will give you the best sense of what they're willing to pay, and will allow you to place yourself within the average competition;

92. How does your desired salary compare with the industry average for this role?

Before a job interview, you have to research and understand what is the average industry salary for your role and seniority.

Of course, different factors may influence it, like geographical location, industry, inflation, taxes, etc.; but at least a range you should have in mind.

Avoid giving round numbers, as it could limit the negotiation; if one party gives a round number, it gives the signal that the party doesn't know what it's doing;

93. Would you be open to relocation?

Remote working is becoming an integral part of a job offer, yet not every company is so future-oriented.

My recommendation is that if you're young and without family implications, spending some years abroad could only increase your wealth of knowledge; which you can then use to better position yourself in the local job market if you decide to go back home.

But even if you are a senior professional with a family, and you'd like to relocate, make sure to negotiate a strong family package (e.g. schooling for your children, house renting, maybe a company car or comprehensive health insurance);

94. What is your current package?

The Interviewers are investigating what is on top of the salary compensation.

Adding fringe benefits to the offer gives fiscal aid to Employers.

For example, accident and health benefits, achievement awards, adoption assistance, athletic facilities, commuting benefits, dependent care assistance, educational assistance, employee discounts, employee stock options, Employer-provided cell phones, group-term life insurance coverage, meals, retirement planning services, tuition reduction, etc.;

95. What is your notice period?

In an employment contract, a notice period is between receiving the letter of dismissal and the end of the last working day.

It is regulated by law and included in your contract; the more years of experience you have, the longer it will be (especially if with the same company).

Before the interview is wise to double-check it with your payroll provider as the Recruiter will certainly want to know;

96. Do you have any questions for us?

Even though coming up with questions can be tricky, it's always better to respond with a question than to politely decline.

Otherwise, you could leave the impression that you're not engaged in the conversation, or that you're not interested enough in the position.

If you're meeting with someone from HR, for instance, your questions might focus on the interviewing process or the overall organization of the company; if you're meeting with HM, you might ask specific questions about your intended role or about the hiring process of new employees.

And remember, getting to the interview stage signifies that you're a top candidate. With thoughtful questions, you can continue to stand out from other contenders and demonstrate that you're a great fit for the role;

i. Embarrassing:

In many countries, laws are implemented to prevent organizations from engaging in discriminatory practices against protected classes when selecting individuals for jobs.

It is normally unlawful for private Employers with 15 or more employees along with state and local Government Employers to discriminate against applicants based on the following: race, colour, sex (including pregnancy), national origin, age (40 or over), disability, or genetic information.

More specifically, an Employer cannot legally "fail or refuse to hire or to discharge any individual, or otherwise discriminate against any individual concerning his compensation, terms, conditions, or privilege of employment" or "to limit, segregate, or classify his employees or applicants for employment in any way which would deprive or tend to deprive any individual of employment opportunities or otherwise adversely affect his status as an employee".

Some examples of embarrassing questions could be:

97. What is your religion?

98. How old are you?

99. What's your sexual orientation?

100. Do you have any serious medical conditions?

101. Are you planning on having children?

The list would be longer, but I'm sure you already got the point.

If you are asked any of the above or similar, do one thing only, take your things and go home.

I don't need to explain to you how to answer them, no job is worth discrimination.

Salary negotiation

In some industries, a weak labour market has left candidates with fewer options and less leverage, and Employers better positioned to dictate terms.

Those unemployed, or whose current job seems not secured, have seen their bargaining power further reduced.

However, the complexity of the job market creates opportunities for people to negotiate the terms and conditions of employment, especially for skilled profiles.

Not everyone is a born negotiator, though.

Like how price-bargaining is an acquired skill, successful negotiation also requires a different mindset.

Most candidates can do more when negotiating for a higher salary, therefore I thought of dedicating a separate section of this guide to salary negotiation.

The first rule when you go into a salary discussion is to never settle for the first salary amount put on the table.

Just because the salary offers feel enough to cover your expenses doesn't necessarily mean it is the market average.

As such, it is critical to do your market research and know what your role is worth before you step into an interview and negotiate for a higher salary.

Glassdoor can surely help with this task.

According to research by American Columbia University, precise offers are potent anchors, you should ask for a specific number rather than a round number in any negotiation.

The research found that when you provide a more precise amount, it implies that you have done more extensive research, and you are more informed of your market value.

You would likely get an offer closer to what you are looking at.

Another point is to consider the full package.

The salary on offer might be lower than the value you have in mind; however, the benefits that come with it might be attractive and more than compensate for the balance.

As a job applicant, you want to consider these additional benefits when negotiating for a raise.

Such as better health plans, retirement planning services, flexible work arrangements, additional leave, training opportunities, athletic facilities or gym memberships, meals, company stocks, company car allowance, etc.

But at the end of the day, salary negotiations have no guarantees.

Beyond the value you can bring to the company, there are many considerations from the Employer, HR points of view, and factors, such as tight budgets and even tighter competition.

Help them understand why you deserve what you're requesting.

It's not enough for them to like you, they also have to believe you're worth the offer you want.

Never let your proposal speak for itself—always tell the story that goes with it.

That said, if you don't even attempt to negotiate salary, you are doing yourself a great disservice in the long run.

So do your research, enter a negotiation, and take the conversation on from there, but please avoid giving ultimatums (they don't work).

Last recommendation

This guide aims to mentor you through the steps of a job interview process and to train you to maximize your chances of getting hired.

Having sat on the Recruiter side for 10 years made my methods proven, not only have I interviewed thousands of candidates from students to Directors, but I have also filled the majority of roles I managed.

However, if you want to be successful, YOU HAVE TO ADD SOMETHING MORE!

My dear reader, I'm sorry if I may disappoint you, but remember that I won't be there with you during the interviews, and most importantly, every selection process is different.

We can't predict every single variable you will encounter, plus the competition is extremely high, therefore you have to do your best.

Don't worry though, we are all unique, and we all have different skills and capabilities; know that if you get rejected for a role, it only means that you will better fit in another.

Never give up, and always try to learn from experiences.

Every experience, positive or negative, has a takeaway, you just have to notice it and channel your reaction.

Finally, keep in mind that if you require some help and guidance, there are professionals who can help.

Go and reach out to the nearest Career Advisor or Job Coach.

From the bottom of my heart, I wish you the best of luck and a very fruitful and satisfying career.

Andrea Masala

Bibliography

- A Great Place to Work for All – Michael C. Bush
- Getting Things Done: The Art of Stress-Free Productivity – David Allen
- The 7 Habits of Highly Effective People – Stephen R. Covey
- Great Work: How to Make a Difference People Love – David Sturt
- Atomic Habits – James Clear
- Start with Why – Simon Sinek
- The Diary of a CEO – Steven Bartlett
- The 4-hour Work Week – Timothy Ferriss
- The Innovator's Dilemma – Clayton M. Christensen
- Great Answers to Tough Interview Questions – Martin John Yate
- Read People Like a Book – Patrick King
- Reinventing You – Dorie Clark
- Switchers: How Smart Professionals Change Careers – David Graham

- The Elephant's Dilemma: Break Free and Reimagine Your Future at Work – Jon Bostock
- Unbreakable: Building and Leading Resilient Teams – Bradley L. Kirkman and Adam Stoverink

Websites

- https://dictionary.cambridge.org/
- https://www.jobtestprep.co.uk/
- https://www.adp.com/
- https://youglish.com/
- https://www.monster.com/
- https://www.michaelpage.com.au/
- https://www.glassdoor.it/
- https://hbr.org/ (Harvard Business Review)
- https://business.linkedin.com/talent-solutions
- https://www.uschamber.com/co/
- https://www.themuse.com/
- https://www.indeed.com/career-advice
- https://knockri.com/
- https://www.wikipedia.org/
- https://www.coursera.org/
- https://www.thebalancemoney.com/
- https://learntocodewith.me/
- https://www.fastcompany.com/
- https://www.bloomberg.com/europe

- https://globalnews.ca/education/
- https://www.forbes.com/
- https://www.greatplacetowork.com/
- https://www.theguardian.com/global-development/employment
- https://asnor.it/
- https://www.comptia.org/home
- https://medium.com/
- https://www.investopedia.com/
- https://novoresume.com/
- https://www.mockquestions.com/
- https://www.keka.com/
- https://careersidekick.com/
- https://insightglobal.com/
- https://economictimes.indiatimes.com/topic/leadership
- https://www.businessinsider.com/?r=US&IR=T
- https://www.economist.com/
- https://www.mindtools.com/
- https://www.smartbrief.com/
- https://www.brightnetwork.co.uk/

My links

Find all my projects and initiatives here:

https://linktr.ee/andreamasala_careerformulas

PS: if you enjoyed this guide, please remember to leave me a review, it is extremely important for me and my project.

Thank you.

Printed in Great Britain
by Amazon